Original title:
The Ocean's Last Call

Copyright © 2025 Creative Arts Management OÜ
All rights reserved.

Author: Dante Kingsley
ISBN HARDBACK: 978-1-80587-459-1
ISBN PAPERBACK: 978-1-80587-929-9

Dusk's Embrace on Water

The sun slips down, a winking eye,
The waves all giggle, oh so spry.
Seagulls wear shades, in quite the flair,
While fish sing tunes, without a care.

A crab recites a silly joke,
As dolphins leap, they start to poke.
With clam shells clapping in great cheer,
They bid the day a loud good cheer.

Songs of the Sea's Sunset

Harmonies rise with the tide's slow sway,
As starfish groove in their curious way.
A sea turtle breaks into a smile,
While seaweed dances, that's their style.

Shells form a band, they play so loud,
Even barnacles join the crowd.
The sunset paints the sky in hues,
But the laughter's what every fish chose.

Crashing Waves of Goodbye

With splashes high, the waves do say,
"Please don't leave us, come back and play!"
They crash and tumble, in playful jest,
While jellyfish wiggle, feeling blessed.

A floating buoy shouts, "Not yet, friend!"
While sea cucumbers start to bend.
The shoreline giggles, it's all in fun,
As twilight whispers, the day is done.

A Salty Breeze at Twilight

The salty breeze tickles the cheeks,
As crabs tell tales that last for weeks.
Starfish giggle, they can't quite stand,
They tumble and roll, across the sand.

A pelican dips, looking for snacks,
While flounders plan their sneaky hacks.
The sun bows low, it's quite the sight,
With the ocean chuckling into the night.

Glimmers of a Distant Memory

Once a fish wore a little hat,
Swam around, looking very fat.
He bumped into a floating log,
And shouted, "Hey! You blocked my fog!"

A crab danced wildly, paused to blink,
While jellyfish giggled, what do you think?
Seagulls cackled from the sandy shore,
"Stop clowning around, we need to soar!"

Watercolors of the Night Sky

Stars painted smiles across the tide,
As sailors tried to play hide and slide.
A whale with shades kept splashing fun,
While mermaids sang, 'Hey, we're number one!'

A gnome on a boat tried fishing for stars,
Instead caught a wave and some candy bars.
Octopi clapped, what a silly sight,
Underneath the glow of moonlight bright!

The End of a Seafarer's Tale

A pirate sat atop a barrel,
His parrot laughed, in a feathered feral.
With a map made of a pizza pie,
He declared, "Sailors stink, oh my, oh my!"

He sought treasure in the cooking pot,
Hoping for gold but found a hot knot.
With a wink to the sun, he gave a cheer,
"A taco feast is my greatest fear!"

Final Voyage Beyond

A sea turtle drove a tiny boat,
With a scarf that seemed to float.
He glanced at dolphins, laughed with glee,
"Join me! We're racing! Who's got the key?"

They zoomed past waves with bubbles of song,
But tripped on seaweed, not for long.
A kraken waved with a coffee cup,
"Did someone order a big ol' sup?"

Tides at Twilight's End

Waves whisper secrets, they tickle my toes,
A crab wearing sunglasses strikes quite a pose.
Seagulls all giggle, they dive for a snack,
While dolphins dance disco, no need to hold back.

The horizon winks, it's a comical sight,
Starfish in tuxedos, they dance with delight.
Shells chatter in rhythms that nobody hear,
As octopuses juggle with not a single fear.

Chronicles of the Distant Horizon

A ship made of pizza sails under the sun,
While sailors sing songs, oh what merry fun!
Fish wear top hats, they swim with such flair,
The turtles are gossiping, without a care.

The mermaids are laughing, a party ensues,
As they mix up potions of seaweed and brews.
Narwhals compare hats, and seahorses prance,
With every wave crashing, they bid life a chance.

Surrendered to the Depths

A whale sings a tune, completely off-key,
While pirates play bingo, they're quite a sight, see?
Barnacles frolic, all dressed up in style,
And fish wear bow ties, they swim with a smile.

Treasure maps scribbled on napkins for fun,
Finding their fortune, oh, what a run!
Anglerfish laugh, they illuminate gloom,
As jellyfish waltz in a shimmering room.

A Farewell to Starry Waters

The stars in the sky all twinkle with cheer,
While ducks in tuxedos parade without fear.
With squawks of delight, they toast with some foam,
Even sea cucumbers are ready to roam.

The waves wave goodbye, a carnival show,
As fish throw confetti, in splendid flow.
A last dance for crabs, who shake with delight,
In the depths of the sea, they part with a bite.

Driftwood Dreams

In a log that floats with grace,
A crab insists on a race.
The seagulls laugh and swoop,
As they plot to steal my soup.

Mermaids braid their seaweed hair,
While dolphins dance without a care.
But watch your step on sandy floor,
Or you might trip and start a roar!

The Retreat of Ancient Waves

Once a wave had quite a quirk,
It tried to surf—oh what a perk!
But tripped upon a stubborn rock,
And splashed the fish, who laughed in shock.

'Come back, dear wave,' the seagulls tease,
'Your surfing skills are quite a breeze!'
With bubbles forming in its wake,
It dodges shells—oh, for fun's sake!

Silenced Shores

On quiet sands where pups dig deep,
The crabs hold council, secrets to keep.
'No more chips or feet in our sandcastles!'
'Let's start a trend with swift prancing gallantles!'

An octopus juggles, quite aloof,
As clams applaud from below the roof.
But who can hear? The laughter is loud,
Our ocean jokes make shells so proud!

Beneath the Brightening Skies

Underneath the skies so bright,
A jellyfish joins the kite in flight.
'Catch me if you can!' it beams,
But turns, and floats for fishy dreams.

The crabs have plans to start a band,
With seashells playing on the sand.
Together we'll sing sea shanties all day,
As the sun sets and the gulls start to play!

The Final Siren's Call

A fish with a hat sings a tune,
While crabs tap dance under the moon.
Seagulls join in with a cawing cheer,
Claiming they're hosts to a raucous beer.

A sailor lost his socks on the shore,
Says he'll never trust seaweed anymore.
Mermaids giggle as they flip their tails,
While octopuses share gossip in gales.

The tide rolls in with a wobbly wave,
Salty snacks floating, oh, what a rave!
Starfish play poker, can't find their cards,
While clams read romance, with all their regards.

As night falls down, the laughter grows loud,
Walruses waltz, drawing quite a crowd.
A boisterous voice shouts, "Oh, let's have fun!"
And so the sea party has just begun!

Deep Blue Goodbyes

A turtle packed bags for a trip afar,
With flip-flops on fins and a beachy guitar.
Dolphins wear shades as they surf through the curls,
While jellyfish throw in some sparkly swirls.

Crabs in a conga line shimmy and sway,
Claiming the shoreline to dance all day.
The seaweed waves as if it can groove,
While seashells shout, "Come on, let's move!"

A whale starts to juggle, using seaweed fronds,
As clowns in the surf blow up frothy ponds.
A fish in a bowtie gives out silly cheers,
Filling the ocean with giggles and jeers.

As the sun dips low, in a splash of gold,
The antics of sea folk are joys to behold.
With fins in the air, they bid their adieu,
On a wave of pure laughter, they sail into blue!

Soliloquy of a Deserted Coast

Upon the shore, a lone crab dances,
In flip-flopped shoes, he takes his chances.
He boasts of treasure, a shiny old spoon,
While seagulls chuckle and waltz to the tune.

Sandcastles crumble like dreams made of fluff,
The tide bursts in laughing, 'That's not enough!'
A flip-flop flies, hits a wayward fish,
He looks up, surprised, 'Not on my wish list!'

Shadows of the Sand

Footprints lead to nowhere, what a merry chase,
The sun takes a selfie with a silly face.
A beach ball tumbles, trying to be cool,
But ends up stuck in a seaweed pool.

A sunburnt hut waves its bright red flag,
As a lost beach towel takes off with a snag.
The ocean whispers jokes as it splashes and rolls,
And each wave is laughing, tickling our souls.

Beneath the Weight of Waves

A squid tries stand-up, but slips on a shell,
The punchline chokes, and he knows it too well.
Starfish cheer loud for their underwater pal,
While jellyfish giggle at the nearby gal.

A dolphin's doing flips, grabs a sunbeam tight,
Yet misjudges the splash and puts out the light.
The seaweed's swaying, tangled in delight,
As bubbles pop with laughter, taking flight.

Last Ripples of the Heart

A rubber duck floats, dreaming of fame,
But the tide rolls in, and forgets his name.
With puffy cheeks, he yells, 'I'm a star!'
While crabs underneath think he's gone too far.

A pair of flip-flops, on a journey quite wild,
Wanders off, leaving behind a lost child.
The beach chair snickers, resting in the sun,
'Life's a lot funnier without anyone!'

A Symphony of Distant Seas

The seagulls sing off-key, quite a treat,
As crabs dance about on tiny feet.
Fish flip and flop, a splashy choir,
While waves clap hands, never tire.

A shell turned trumpet, a clam's sweet sound,
Jellyfish waltz 'round, not a clue they're round.
Octopuses juggle, what a sight to see,
While the starfish wonders, 'Hey, is that me?'

Shattered Reflections in Saltwater

Mirrors of sea, reflecting the sky,
But narwhals posing look a bit shy.
Turtles in sun hats, shades on their eyes,
Debating if it's better to swim or to fly.

Sand on their faces, oh what a mess!
Seashells debating their fashion, no less.
With flippers for feet, they dance on the shore,
While crabs gossip about the fish's galore.

Fading Echoes of the Coast

A dolphin giggles, leaps to the sun,
While barnacles plot, 'Now that looks fun!'
With sandcastles crumbling, they cheer with glee,
"Next time, let's build one that's taller than me!"

Seashells are snickering, stuck on the sand,
Wondering why mermaids don't find them so grand.
Anemones chuckle, all tucked in their beds,
As crabs trade their gossip, a few loose threads.

Transitory Tides

The tide rolls in with much pomp and flair,
While fish play peek-a-boo, unaware.
Starfish wave goodbye, then change their minds,
"I'll stay a while longer, see what one finds!"

Seagulls make bets on who dives the best,
While sea cucumbers lounge, taking a rest.
With laughter and splashes, it's quite a parade,
Even the crabs have come out, unafraid!

Unmoored Emotions at Dusk

As seagulls squawk, my sandwich flies,
Tuna tornadoes in the sky.
A crab in a tux, all dressed to chill,
Waltzing off with my fries at will.

The tides are in for a dance tonight,
Drunken shells swirl, all silly and bright.
Castles I built now look like soup,
While jellyfish jive in a wobbly loop.

Fish wear sunglasses, kings of the sea,
"Can you lend me a fin?" they chuckle with glee.
Octopus juggling, so hard to impress,
Who knew they'd be better at this than I guess?

But as sun dips low, it's time to go,
My beach ball's lost; it's a sinking low.
With one last wave, and a splash of foam,
I bid my goodbyes to this sandy home.

Ephemeral Horizons

A dolphin debated fashion all day,
In polka dots, it swam for a play.
Mermaids giggled, with hair made of sea,
Trying to style the waves; all while sipping tea.

Surfboards that skateboarded into a craze,
All wishing for the perfect sun rays.
Crabs with sunglasses on their claws,
Strutting the beach without any flaws.

The shells held meetings on who wore best,
Talking nonsense, like all of the rest.
Sharks took selfies, flexing their teeth,
While whales serenaded beneath the wreath.

As dusk comes in, there's laughter and cheer,
Chasing sunsets, without any fear.
I wave goodbye to this carnival fun,
As the stars start winking; the laughter has won.

The Silent Horizon's Denouement

Once a walrus tried to hop on a boat,
Fell off, started a seafood float.
The crabs were judges in a slapstick crime,
As plankton performed for the audience prime.

Seashells whispered juicy gossip all night,
"Did you hear what the squid said to the kite?"
Fetch a bucket; I hear the clownfish sing,
While starfish argue over who is the king.

Tangs in tutus twirl in the foam,
While beach balls bounce in their watery dome.
Flip-flops argue over whose is whose,
In this bizarre, underwater ruse.

With laughter lingered on a salty breeze,
I skip a stone, aim for tall palm trees.
The horizon smiles as dusk bows down,
To the ocean's antics and the sea's silly crown.

Waves of Yesterday

An otter mixed lemonade with the tide,
Juggling coconuts, full of pride.
A clam's singing loudly, but out of tune,
Echoes of mischief under a cheerful moon.

Starfish contemplate their lifelong goals,
Deciding if they should play, or just scroll.
Meanwhile, a pufferfish joins the jam,
Spitting bubbles like a little ham.

Penguins imitate a dolphin's leap,
While seals are napping, in a quiet heap.
Seashells gossip about old tides,
Riding the current with their playful sides.

The sun sets low; it's time to unwind,
Counting all the giggles, so perfectly timed.
As the day fizzles out and the sea turns gray,
I'll cherish the laughter of yesterday's play.

Beneath the Bleeding Sky

A crab in a tux, ready to dance,
He twirls and he spins, in a sideways prance.
A fish wearing shades, looks quite the sight,
Says, "I'm off to a rave, under the moonlight!"

The seaweed whispers jokes to the waves,
While dolphins play poker, like a bunch of braves.
A shark with a top hat, quite dapper and keen,
Calls out, "Who's up for some seashell cuisine?"

The sun is a ketchup, splattered on blue,
Each wave's a potato, in a stew for a crew.
A clam tells the tale of a ship that ate gravel,
"Next time bring snacks, it's a long, long travel!"

A seagull calls out with a deep belly laugh,
"Dive into the tide, come join my fun bath!"
But the fish just roll eyes, "Not again with this jest,
Last time we ended up in a seagull fest!"

Ghosts of the Mariner's Heart

A ghost with a parrot, lost in a fog,
Sings sea shanties loud, while chasing a dog.
The tail-wagging phantom, a sight to behold,
Kept barking for treasure, or maybe for gold?

A ship sails past with a crew full of jest,
They're looking for trouble, but they found a rest.
With humor so bright, even the anchors would cheer,
As the wind filled their sails with a giggle and beer.

The captain's a skeleton, with a hook for a hand,
His jokes about fishing were simply not grand.
Said, "I lost my arm fighting a tuna at sea,
But don't worry, it swam back to fight me, you see?"

With laughter like thunder, they haunt through the night,
Pirates and phantoms in shimmering light.
In a twisted old boat, they play tag with the tides,
While dreaming of snacks on their ghostly rides.

Reflections of a Sinking Sun

The sun in the water, like ketchup on fries,
Reflecting in giggles, with winking goodbyes.
The waves do a shimmy, all splashes and spark,
Chasing dark shadows that glide through the park.

A seal tells a tale of a balloon on a trip,
It floated away, and gave a big whip.
The fishes all chuckle, as they dance all around,
"More balloons, please! Let our parties abound!"

A pirate in flip-flops is searching for rum,
While a mermaid plays tunes on a whimsical drum.
"Where did my treasure map go?" he sighed in lament,
"It's buried in sand, or perhaps at a tent?"

The sun starts to sink, in a candy-floss hue,
With giggles and bubbles, it ends this night too.
And the sea laughs along, as day says farewell,
With secrets of laughter that no one could tell.

Where the Sea Meets the Silence

Where laughter erupts in the deep blue expanse,
The gulls take the stage for a perfect romance.
"Who needs a shore? We've got awkward dance moves!
Come join in the fun, let's see who can groove!"

A crab with a bow tie, all posh and bemused,
Declares, "I'm a star! Look, I'm not even bruised!"
While fishes spin tales of a giant old squid,
"His name is Fred, and he hums when he's hid!"

The waves clap their hands to the music they hear,
With conch shells as drums, echoing loud and clear.
As tide rolls away, the applause fills the air,
For a show that was silly, but we couldn't care!

As the sun gives a wink, painting gold on the sea,
All join in the fun, shouting "Come dance with me!"
In this splashy world where the wild times prevail,
Even silence holds laughter; it's a comical tale.

Tidal Farewells

The seagulls shout their goodbyes,
While sand crabs dance with great surprise.
A dolphin twirls, a splashy show,
"See ya later!" — off they go.

The waves roll in, a comic race,
A fish gives chase, it's quite a chase.
A beach ball sighs, it's time to leave,
"I'll miss my friends!" it moans, naive.

The starfish waves with little arms,
It's ready to ditch those beachy charms.
With flip-flops flying in the air,
They giggle and leap without a care.

As tides retreat with a silly grin,
The seashells laugh, their jokes begin.
"What's the ocean's favorite snack?"
"A crab sandwich, now that's a fact!"

Closure of Oceanic Journeys

The sunset paints the sea with jokes,
While seals put on their finest coats.
A whale hums tunes of far-off lands,
While sea turtles strike their silly stands.

The sandcastles begin to frown,
As night creeps in, they tumble down.
"Not fair! We built this brick by brick!"
But waves just laugh, "You're quite a trick!"

The crabs gather for a final show,
Tap dancing wildly, putting on a glow.
With clapping claws, and shells that shine,
They cheer, "This ocean was divine!"

As stars twinkle bright in the deep blue,
They whisper, "Good night; we'll miss you!"
The tides may shift, but who needs rest?
For ocean antics are truly the best!

Memories Lost in Currents

A bottle floats with a cheeky grin,
"Send help!" it shouts, like it's in a spin.
Inside, a note with a silly plot,
"Oops, I spilled my drink—oh, what a lot!"

The fish parade flaunts their best attire,
With glittery scales, they dance like fire.
"Oh look! A crab!" they giggle and tease,
"He's just a diva, trying to please!"

As mermaids laugh and lose their crowns,
"An ocean trip with no boats around!"
Their laughter echoes, waves start to sigh,
"Dive deep for fun, don't pass us by!"

The tide retreats with a yawning cheer,
"Keep those memories close and near!"
As fish swim off, with a playful dive,
"Remember us, as we stay alive!"

Sinking Whispers

A sunken ship begins to sing,
With rusty notes it claims the bling.
"Once I sailed with sails so grand,
Now I'm a home for fish and sand!"

Bubbles laugh as they float away,
Carrying secrets of a salty day.
"Tell me a tale," they giggle and squeak,
"About storms that turned the sea so bleak!"

The octopus winks, in a playful jest,
"Who needs a map? Let's just quest!"
With tentacles flailing in sunset hues,
"What's your story? Come share the news!"

Whispers drift in the currents' swirl,
Fish swap tales, let spontaneity unfurl.
In deep blue depths, with laughter in tow,
The sea's true beauty, the giggles will flow!

Ballad of the Fading Brine

The fish in flippers waltz away,
As waves forget to dance and play.
Seagulls bend to the salty breeze,
Chasing crabs who taste the tease.

With lobster hats and jelly shoes,
The treasure maps are full of clues.
But fish are laughing, what a sight,
In waters dimming out of fright.

A clam once held a gossip fest,
Tales of pirates on a quest.
But sharks just yawn, they've lost their thrill,
And surfboards ride on phantom still.

So raise a glass of seaweed tea,
To tides that swell with glee, you see!
Let's toast to days of brighter blue,
Before the shore bids us adieu!

Serenity in the Sea's Embrace

The crabs have taken up ballet,
As seaweed sways without a care.
A starfish dons a polka dot,
While fishes rant about their spot.

Barnacles, they throw a bash,
With dancing shells and sea-moss stash.
But every wave brings tales of gloom,
As dolphins plot to leave the room.

The mermaids knit with tangled nets,
Making hats for their pet pets.
And with a wink, the sun dips low,
To tease the fish "You're too slow!"

Yet laughter bubbles through the foam,
In salty homes, the sea's their home.
With giddy tides as friends, they sing,
And pray the tide brings back the spring!

Remnants of a Watery Realm

In coral castles, fish still pout,
As waters shallow more about.
They reminisce with fishy tears,
And start to plan a land of cheers.

The otters trade their shells for gold,
While seahorses get very bold.
They play a game of underwater ball,
Till sea trees whisper, "That's all!"

An octopus with paint so bright,
Draws mustaches on a whale's sight.
But as the tide begins to wane,
They sigh, "We'll have to ride the train."

The tides may fade, the laughs may cease,
Yet ocean creatures seek their peace.
With jokes and jives, they bid farewell,
To remnants of their liquid spell.

The Conch's Dying Whistle

The conch once sent out deep, loud calls,
Now whispers secrets, as ocean stalls.
"I swear I heard a whale's sad tune,"
But now it's just a silver spoon.

The crab choir sings off-key for fun,
While jellyfish play with the setting sun.
The sea turtles wear snorkels and dive,
To find out if sea life can survive.

A hermit crab's got quite a joke,
He hides his shell while eating smoke.
The sea anemone rolls its eyes,
"Oh please, I'm not surprised!"

With shells that chatter, loud and full,
The underwater party just won't pull.
So let's enchant the swells anew,
For laughter echoes in the blue!

Forgotten Shores

Upon the beach, I found a shoe,
Its mate was lost, where skies are blue.
A crab in anger claimed a spot,
While seagulls squawked, they'd eat the lot.

A sandcastle, proud, began to tilt,
As waves approached with frothy guilt.
The tide came in, the castle fled,
Now just a lump where dreams once spread.

A dolphin danced, thought it was slick,
Until it slipped—what a funny trick!
Fish giggled loud at their dolphin friend,
'The show was great, but it must end!'

So here we sit, as seaweed flies,
Collecting shells and ridiculous ties.
On forgotten shores where laughter sings,
Who needs a thing, when joy it brings?

Lullabies of the Driftwood

Driftwood sings a silly tune,
To crabs who dance beneath the moon.
A clam, half-open, whispers low,
'Is that the wind or a funny show?'

A starfish winks with all its might,
Says, 'I've got stars all day and night!'
The sea turtles bop without a care,
Probably wondering what's out there.

The waves are giggling more each hour,
As barnacles form a tiny tower.
Shells chatter 'bout the latest trend,
'The bigger the shell, the cooler the blend!'

So let the tide roll in, don't fear,
The lullabies for all to hear.
With driftwood dreams that come to play,
We laugh our worries all away!

Solace in the Emptiness

In empty tides, a rubber duck,
Floats by a fish, who's out of luck.
The seagulls strike up quite a band,
With seaweed instruments, oh so grand.

A jellyfish with arms all wide,
Sways gently, but inside it sighed.
'Why can't I dance, like those in bounds?'
Yet still it glows amidst the sounds.

The ocean's deep yet funny too,
Each creature boasts a quirky view.
Fish swap tales of human woe,
As waves roll in, they steal the show.

In emptiness, we find a joke,
Of salty sun and a seaweed cloak.
So here we laugh, until we drop,
In solace, swirling—never stop!

Ebbing Dreams Beneath the Surface

Beneath the waves, a fish named Dave,
Invents a game called 'Brave or Wave.'
With bubbles blown, they start to play,
    Until a crab joins in the fray.

A treasure chest with socks inside,
Said, 'These are gifts from those who tried!'
Seashells laugh and roll around,
'Who knew treasures could be so sound?'

The octopus, with varied hats,
Puts on a show for laughing chats.
Whimsical and full of glee,
    'Look at me, I'm fancy free!'

So as they ebb and flow away,
These dreams beneath come out to play.
Join the fun and let it last,
In ocean's depths, we'll have a blast!

Last Light on the Sand

The sun dips low, a golden crown,
Crabs doing the tango, they won't back down.
Seagulls squawk like they own the place,
While beach balls soar with a cheeky grace.

With each wave's laugh, a splash takes flight,
Seashells whisper secrets of the night.
Surfers wipe out, and the crowd erupts,
While sunscreen scents mix, laughter corrupts.

Tiny fish giggle in watery spree,
Making faces at folks who just can't see.
A flip-flop flies, caught in the breeze,
As sunburned tourists are lost at ease.

But as twilight falls, the jokes get deep,
Mermaids chuckle, as sailors creep.
In shadows they plan for one last jest,
'Til morning wakes them from their quest.

Glistening Tears of the Sea

Waves glimmer like glitter on a misshaped cake,
Fish wearing hats, oh what a mistake!
Octopus juggling shells with glee,
As dolphins dance, 'Look, it's me!'

A crab in a hammock, chilling too long,
Making up tunes to a waterlogged song.
Seashells gossip and trade their tales,
Of beachside picnics and runaway snails.

The tide rolls in, and seaweed is thrown,
On a beach towel, it's now a garden grown.
As laughter bubbles from salty lips,
Every wave a story, every wave a flip.

All the fish are clearly in on this joke,
As the sun sets down, it's time to soak.
Wipe that smudge of laughter from your cheek,
Tomorrow brings joy, but today's the peak.

Wistful Wishes on the Wind

Kites in the sky, they flail and play,
Dreams that float terribly far away.
Sandcastles crumble with a giggling sound,
While whispers of wishes whirl all around.

Seashells wish on the waves' loud cheer,
That time would pause, and mermaids appear.
Children with buckets, so bright and bold,
Searching for treasures, stories untold.

With each puff of breeze, a shared delight,
As gulls play tag, oh what a sight!
Banana peels slip, adults take a dive,
While sandy toes wiggle, feeling alive.

As dusk settles down, what do we see?
Stars dip their toes in that giggling sea.
The ocean's sweet grin unravels the fun,
Tomorrow's adventures already begun.

Where Time Meets Water

Tick-tock, the clock, right by the shore,
Time does a cartwheel, comes back for more.
Jellyfish jelly, quirky and bright,
While sea cucumbers get into a fight.

A buoy in the breeze, bobbing along,
Waves swirl around, singing a song.
Old driftwood chuckles at all who pass,
Claiming it's bolder than any old glass.

Pelicans strut like they own the parade,
Judging the fish with a grand charade.
As hours roll by in a splashy spree,
Every tick makes room for a fishy decree.

As stars begin to twinkle and shout,
The night gathers laughter without a doubt.
For as time meets water, the jestiest fun,
Is a memory made, 'til the new day is done.

Twilight Reflections on Waves

The seagulls dance on the golden sand,
Pretending to be a rock band.
Surfboards fly, oh what a sight,
As surfers battle waves from left to right.

The sunset paints the sky in hues,
While crabs play tag, dodging shoes.
Fish gossip as they swim in a line,
Whispering jokes in bubbles of brine.

A dolphin wears a top hat so grand,
While jellyfish jive, oh isn't it planned?
The seaweed sways like it's in a trance,
Inviting us all for a weird ocean dance.

So grab your floaties, let's join the spree,
In waves of laughter, wild and free.
The tide may call, but don't take it serious,
For every last splash is downright curious!

The Closing Tide

As seagulls squawk on a patchwork sky,
A clam attempts to learn how to fly.
Turtles in sunglasseswaddle ashore,
Yelling, "Hey dude, who ordered more?"

The shore is now strewn with flip-flops,
While barnacles sing out, "Who wants some chops?"
An octopus sneezes, what a surprise!
Sending seaweed flying through summer skies.

Sharks wear a frown, missing their boats,
While swimmers munch on salty oats.
Crabs have a ballet and dance on a log,
Their pirouettes bring laughs, oh what a fog!

So wave goodbye, as the tide turns slow,
With laughter echoing, putting on a show.
The sand will giggle and the waves will roar,
As we leave the beach with tales to explore!

Farewell of the Seafoam

The waves joke gently, with frothy caps,
As sea snails brag about their tiny naps.
"Watch me" one shouts, "I'm quite the spry!
I'll race you to the rock, oh my, oh my!"

The starfish mock with their silly flips,
While anemones dance with the water's drips.
A clam checks its shell, all shiny and bling,
While crabs polish tools for a garden fling.

The ocean waves wave a teasing farewell,
To beachgoers who've stories to tell.
A fish in a tux stands guard by the pier,
Announcing, "Make way, for the pufferfish cheer!"

So laugh with the tide as it rolls on by,
With giggles and splashes, oh my, oh my!
The last of the foam gives a wink and a grin,
As we pack our bags, letting the fun begin!

Lament of the Briny Blue

Oh salty waves, you're a riot today,
With barnacles singing the blues in dismay.
The tide's trying hard to capture a tune,
While seahorses wiggle like they're in a cartoon.

Flotsam and jetsam, a drama unfolds,
With hermit crabs swapping their stories bold.
"Dude, I saw a dolphin with a pink feather,"
Exclaims one crab, chuckling, "A comedian's tether!"

The whales play bingo, calling out loud,
While sardines form a teenage crowd.
"Let's make a meme!" they shriek with a laugh,
As currents twist into a digital gaffe.

So here's to the ocean, with its hilarious charms,
A place where laughter enchants and warms.
With mischievous waves setting rhythms anew,
We bid adieu to the blue, oh what a view!

When Stars Fall into the Sea

The stars decided to take a dive,
Splashing about, oh what a jive!
They giggled and twirled, in the moonlight's glow,
Saying, "Watch us shimmer, put on a show!"

The fish all laughed, saying, "What's this mess?"
Starfish and twinklers in a cosmic dress.
They dove with style, with grace and cheer,
Creating waves of laughter, loud and clear.

But then they found, with a twist so sly,
That swimming's tough when you're all up high.
With fins and sparkles, they tried once more,
Flipping and flopping, like never before!

So if you swim beneath the night sky,
And see a starfish leap, soaring high,
Just know it's a star from the Milky Way,
Making waves and laughter, in a funny way!

Reveries of the Abandoning Shore

The crab played tunes on a conch shell horn,
He waved at seagulls who looked quite worn.
"Hey! Join my band!" the little crab cried,
As hermit crabs danced, nothing to hide.

The waves rolled in, with a silly clap,
"Don't let them fool you, they're just bad at rap!"
But shells kept spinning, in a sandy whirl,
Creating a concert where fish would twirl.

A clam wore glasses, looking quite grand,
While octopuses formed a cool band.
With eight-armed moves, they rocked that sand bar,
Turning the beach into a grand VR!

But as the sun set, there came a surprise,
The tide took the stage—crabs shouted, "Oh, why?"
Through splashes and laughter, the night turned bright,
A party in bubbles, a true seaside delight!

Twilight's Reef

Twilight fell on a sleepy reef,
Fish cracked jokes, oh what a belief!
"Why did the turtle cross the sea?
To show it was faster—can't catch me!"

Coral stood bright in oranges and pink,
A clownfish pondered, "What do you think?"
"I think it's time for a coral parade!"
They danced in the waves, all colorful displayed.

Starfish joined in, with rhythm so neat,
Dancing like stars on their squishy feet.
"If we keep this up, we'll start a trend!"
They laughed, they twirled, no need to pretend.

Then shadows approached, what could it be?
Just dolphins arriving, pure jubilee.
With flips and splashes, they joined the fun,
Twilight's reef reveling 'til night was done!

The Last Breath of Coral

The coral once gasped, 'I need a SPA!',
Bubble massages, and warm sea, hurrah!
"Can someone help with these pesky little fish?"
They piled on top, a slippery squish!

With anemones giggling, watching the fuss,
The fish looked around, and burst into cuss.
"Why do we bother to swim in this space?"
When all we get is an algae embrace?"

Yet as the coral sighed, a plan took flight,
"Let's host a bash! Come revel tonight!"
So all gathered close, with glitter and flair,
In the depths of the sea, they made quite the pair.

And there in the darkness, they found their groove,
For nothing like laughter could help them move.
And though the coral might gasp with dismay,
It learned how to party in a wacky way!

Sheltering Waves of Silence

A whale danced by in a tutu bright,
With a splish and a splash, he took flight.
Fish all giggled, doing the wave,
Once majestic, now slightly rave.

Seagulls squawked in a karaoke night,
While crabs clapped in sheer delight.
They formed a band with shells for drums,
Singing tunes of ocean's funny slums.

The jellyfish glowed like neon signs,
While barnacles spoke in cheesy lines.
"Why did the wave fall flat on the shore?"
"Because it didn't know how to encore!"

In the sandcastles, the starfish grinned,
As the tide rolled back, they all chinned.
Together they laughed at the sea's own jest,
In this frothy world, they felt truly blessed.

Fading Horizons

The sun wore shades while it took a dip,
A beach ball bounced, causing a blip.
Fish surfed waves on inflatable toys,
Squeaking and slipping, oh such noisy boys!

Clouds shaped like ice cream, oh what a treat,
The ocean sighed, feeling the heat.
Crabs offered bug spray for a sunburned back,
While dolphins giggled in a splashy attack.

A clam opened wide, sharing secrets, you know,
"What did the fish say when it's in a show?"
"I'm hooked on the spotlight, just here to reel!"
And everyone laughed at that undersea deal.

As twilight whispered, the antics drew near,
Octopuses juggled, bringing great cheer.
The waves chuckled softly; the night wore its crown,
In this comical sea, no one would frown.

The Final Curl of Foam

A seal in a top hat danced with flair,
While crabs competed in a prancy affair.
They spun and they twirled on smooth, wet sand,
With a flip and a flop, they made their grandstand.

Frogs on surfboards hip-hopped in glee,
While a clam gave commentary on live TV.
"What's green and bouncy and loves the sea?"
"Tadpoles on a vacation, can't you see?"

As bubbles burst, jokes floated in air,
A whale told tales with flair and rare scare.
"Why was the sea so salty, my friend?"
"Because it lost its sea-shell phone, no end!"

So the tide tickled toes and laughter rang out,
Under the moonlight, there's no room for doubt.
With each wave receding, a story is spun,
In this silly haven, the giggles are never done!

Autumn's Whisper on the Waves

The leaves did a conga on the sand so bright,
While sea turtles joined in with all their might.
Singing, "We're not ready to say goodbye,"
They surfed on their shells 'neath the pastel sky.

The crabs wore sweaters, all snuggled and warm,
With beach bonfire stories, they kept out of harm.
"Why did autumn bring a blanket?" they'd pose,
"To keep the beach cozy as the cool wind blows!"

Starfish played poker, shells as their chips,
Counting their winnings with wiggly flips.
"Why trust an octopus with your card?" they would jest,
"Because he has so many plans, and he knows what's best!"

With waves whispering secrets, guilt-free they tread,
As the seasons unfurl, no reason for dread.
For here at the shore, life's a joyful brawl,
As the sea holds its laughter in each rolling thrall!

Epilogue of the Marine Dream

The fish wore hats, it was quite a sight,
Doing the cha-cha, oh what a night!
Seagulls tell jokes, oh how they squawk,
While crabs pull pranks on a drifting dock.

A whale shared secrets, with a wobbly grin,
While turtles played poker beneath their skin.
Jellyfish bounced, like balloons in a fair,
What a crazy party, with salt in the air!

Octopuses dancing, eight legs in a twist,
With rubbery moves, who could resist?
A clam with a glint, like a pirate's gold,
Tales of the depths, silently bold!

So here's to the waves, as they giggle and splash,
With mermaids who belly flop, oh what a crash!
In dreams of the sea, where laughter flows free,
This marine epilogue is just for me!

Whispers of the Tides

The tides are gossiping, what a riddle,
They chuckle and giggle, then play the fiddle.
A starfish spills tea, on a lazy shore,
While sand dollars dance, who could ask for more?

Seahorses prance in a synchronized show,
While floating seaweed waves hi and hello!
Anemones poke, but with ticklish glee,
Leaving fish rolling, in waves of the sea.

Crabs in tuxedos, with top hats askew,
Hold a court session, just for me and you.
They dispute the shell findings, with fervor and flair,
While gulls on the sidelines just drop their despair.

The sea whispers jokes, as it ebbs and it flows,
With a wink and a nudge, anything goes!
So let us listen close, as the waves huddle tight,
In whispers of fun, through the sparkling night.

Farewell to the Horizon

The sun dips low, with a wink and a smile,
A lobster waves goodbye, staying a while.
Fish throw a party till the stars take their seat,
While dolphins cartwheel, with jubilant feet.

Clams hold an auction for pearls shining bright,
George the great grouper bids with delight!
Seashells are prizes, picked with great care,
As waves bring the laughter, floating in air.

Seagulls are silly, with their loud, silly calls,
Making a racket as twilight befalls.
But wave after wave, they begin to unwind,
In this ocean farewell, nothing left behind.

So let's raise a toast, to the night on the sea,
With fish in tuxedos and glee guaranteed.
We'll dream of horizons, with laughter and light,
Saying farewell to the day, under twinkling night.

Echoes Beneath the Waves

Bubbles are echoing, giggles abound,
Underwater parties, silliness found.
Fish tease the sharks, play hide-and-go-seek,
With tickles from eels, oh isn't that chic!

Crabs make a band, with shells for a drum,
While squids do the limbo—oh, how they thrum!
Mollusks join in, with a lovely ballet,
Creating a scene that will steal the whole day.

Seahorses spin with their tails in a knot,
A flag of bright colors—a polka dot!
The whispering waves hold stories anew,
With laughter that dances, and brightly shines through.

So cast off your worries, let joy be your guide,
Join this frolicsome tide, let your heart be the ride.
In echoes beneath, where the merriment sways,
The sea keeps on laughing, through all of our days.

www.ingramcontent.com/pod-product-compliance
Lightning Source LLC
Chambersburg PA
CBHW060147230426
43661CB00003B/604